Locked Out!

A Story of the Prince

Edward County School

Closings

Jamantha Williams Watson

About the Author

It was a Tuesday afternoon, the class had just come in from recess. The temperature in Buffalo, New York was frigid that day; as snow fell in heavy clumps. It was the perfect time to write an essay. While sitting in Ms. Mumm's English class, Jamantha Watson wrote her first short story. "My Family's Camping Adventures" detailed her family's hiking trip into the Alleghany Mountains. Not only did Watson's English teacher find the story amusing, her classmates did as well. Writing and reading that story peaked an interest in storytelling.

A voracious reader, by eighth grade Watson had devoured nearly all of the children's books and plays in the Buffalo Public Library. She has enjoyed consuming gazillions of books since then. At a young age her parents instilled the importance of both writing and reading and the incredible nourishment they add to an individual's overall development.

One of Jamantha Watson's most inspiring quotes was written by Dr. Seuss. "You have brains in your head. You have feet in your shoes. You can steer yourself any direction you choose."

"We may observe with much sadness and irony that, outside of Africa, south of the Sahara, where education is still a difficult challenge, the only places on earth known not to provide free public education are Communist China, North Viet Nam, Sarawak, Singapore, British Honduras – and Prince Edward County, Virginia. Something must be done about Prince Edward County."

- Robert F. Kennedy
March 18, 1963
at the Kentucky Centennial of the
Emancipation Proclamation

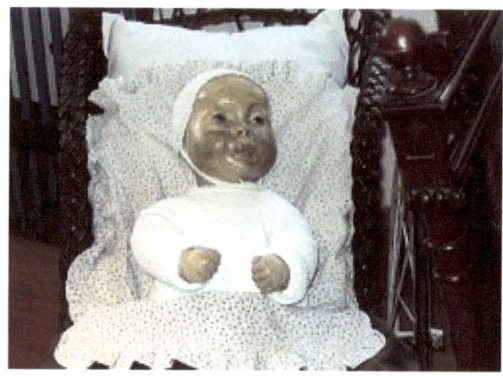

Learline opened her eyes, then shut them tight. She slid the cozy blanket down her forehead, over her nose and underneath her chin. Blinking, she looked around the room. Even in the near dark bedroom she could see that everything still looked as it had before she'd gone to bed the night before. Her clothes were neatly folded on the chair beside the dresser, her shoes rested in the middle of the floor and her doll baby, Clara Mae, slept quietly beside her.

Everything looks the same she thought, but today is very different. Very, very different.

Learline hopped out of bed, slipped on her house shoes and ran down the hallway to the kitchen.

"Good morning everybody. Today is a big day. Today is the first day of school."

Her daddy bit a corner off the triangled piece of toast and smiled at her. "Morning back at you, doll baby."

"Good morning sugar," her mother smiled, blowing into her steaming cup of coffee before sipping it. "You'd better come sit down for breakfast before you go talking about going off to school this morning. Aunt Rose has made you a big breakfast; so big there's enough here to feed six hungry men. And I don't know why she cooked up so much food this morning, anyhow."

"Oh Bessie, stop your complaining now," Aunt Rose said, walking across the kitchen, setting a bowl on the countertop, then turning off the radio, "Auntie only has one little darling, and I intend to spoil her for as long as I'm down here in Virginia. Besides Bessie, you've got to eat some more yourself. You've got two little ones on the way. You're eating for three now. You know?"

Aunt Rose placed her hands on Learline's face and kissed her cheek. "Isn't that right Sugar Plum?"

Learline grinned up at Aunt Rose, "Yes ma'am.

"Now," Aunt Rose tilted her head, "what's so special about today young lady,"

"Auntie," Learline giggled, "you know. It's my first day of school today. I'm a big girl now," she exclaimed.

"Oh boy," Aunt Rose winked at Learline's mommy and daddy, "is that right?"

"Yes ma'am. And we're going to learn the ABC's and play games, and the teacher is going to tell us stories and we're going to have lots, and lots, and lots of fun in school today."

"Oh boy! Well I guess you'd better go on and eat that big breakfast then. Sounds like you have a mighty big day in front of you," her aunt laughed. "Let's see now, I've whipped up some pancakes, sausages and bacon. I fried up some apples and scrambled up those eggs just like you like them. Been away from the south for a couple of years, but I still haven't lost my touch for some good old down home cooking."

"Amen to that," Learline's daddy said, placing a forkful of pancakes in his mouth.

"Yummy," Learline plopped down at the breakfast table and grinned. "I can't wait to eat all of my food. And I can't wait to put on all my pretty school clothes. Just can't

wait to…"

"Don't you want to say the blessing first?" her

daddy asked.

"Oh, that's right."

"Well," her mother smiled, "maybe you should go

in the bathroom and wash those pretty little hands before

you dig in to such a big breakfast. Huh?"

"Yes ma'am."

"Rose, why are you getting her all riled up like that this morning?" Learline heard her daddy ask Aunt Rose.

"Booker," Aunt Rose whispered, "that baby has a gleam in her eyes so bright about the first day of school, there is no way in the world I'm going to put it out by letting her know what a few foolish crazy people think about her and her education."

"Well Rose," her mother said, "now Booker is right, no matter how crazy it sounds. They've been talking about it on the radio all summer long. And we all know that they're not going to open the schools back up this year for our children; maybe for theirs, but not for ours."

"Ummm hmm," her daddy agreed.

"Those white folk are not even going to let their own children get an education; so you know they're not thinking about ours."

"It's a crying shame."

"Seems like they would make some kind of arrangements for their own children; even if they don't want to make arrangements for ours."

"Well that's 'cause that would be too much like right. These white folk down here in Prince Edward County, Virginia would rather have their own children go without any education at all before they let them sit side by side with our children in the same classroom. Colored folk and white folk mix worse than oil and water. "

"It's a crying shame, is what it really is."

"Who are you telling? "

"Don't I know it?"

"And that's the very reason I had to leave all of this evil racism right down here in Virginia. Folk don't behave so much like devils up north," said Aunt Rose.

"Yeah well just because those white folk up there in New York City don't behave the same way as these white folk do down here in Prince Edward County, doesn't mean they're not all thinking the same way."

"Now that's the truth," Learline heard her Aunt Rose agreeing with her mother and father.

Just then, holding the bar of soap in her hand, Learline didn't feel so hungry anymore. Instead, she felt full; ready to burst into a flood of tears.

Even though Learline couldn't understand all of the big words the adults were putting beside their small words, she had a good feeling that all the whispering meant she wouldn't be going to school that day.

But did they really mean she wouldn't be able to go to school at all; forever?   Or just not today?

She pulled the towel from the wall and wiped her hands on it, then tossed it in the sink. Slowly, she walked back into the kitchen with her family.

Staring up at her mother, her daddy and her Aunt Rose, Learline could tell by the looks on their faces, they knew she had heard their whispers.

"Mommy," she whined, "why can't I go to school today?"

"Sweetie," her mother smiled. "We don-."

"No one is saying for certain that you're not going to school today sugar plum. We just have to wait and see," Aunt Rose added, "that's all."

"Rose," Learline's daddy looked sideways at her aunt.

"Well Booker, what do you want me to say?"

"I'm just saying that we shouldn't get the child all worked up about something that we ourselves know is not going to happen," her daddy explained. "These white folk around here aren't even opening the schools for their own children, let alone ours.

"And if we sit back and believe everything white folks say, we'll all be in a world of trou-."

"Rose," Learline's mother interrupted, "white folks are the ones making the rules in this town, not us. We can figure something else out about Learline's schooling, when the time comes."

"Like what? What else can we figure out about our baby's education Bessie?" Her daddy asked. "Schools are supposed to start today in Prince Edward."

"If nothing else," Aunt Rose patted Bessie's shoulder, "Learline can always go back with me and live up north.

They have good schools in New York. I teach in one of the

best schools in Harlem. Y'all know that. The good Lord

knows Learline can come and visit y'all down here

as much as she wants to, and my home is always open to

the both of you."

Sliding down in her chair, Learline bowed her head, folded her hands and closed her eyes.

"Dear Lord, please let me be able to go to school today. Please let the white folk open up the schools for all of us; the colored and the white. Thank you Lord. Amen. Oh, and Jesus please let my mommy have two brand new baby girls real soon. And let me be able to play with them here in my own house, every day. And nowhere else. Amen."

"Amen," her family chimed.

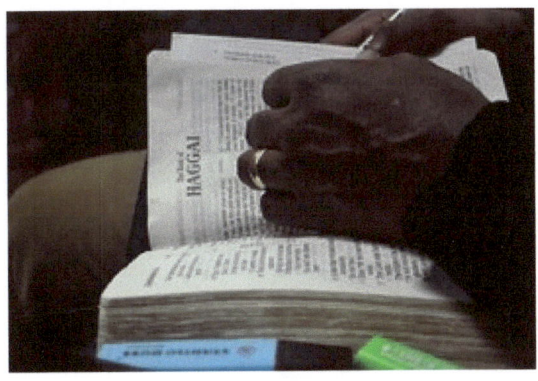

Aunt Rose brushed her hands over her lap and stood, "Well, we might as well eat up all of this good food," she said, placing a few pieces of bacon and sausage and some eggs and toast on a plate for Learline, "no need in letting it get cold."

"But I don't feel like eating; since I'm not going to school today," Learline mumbled, looking up at her mother. "Do I have to?"

Her mother looked down at her and smiled. "Just drink your milk baby. Ok?"

"Ok," she sulked.

"Well little lady," her daddy said, "if you're not going to eat anything at all this morning, you may as well go on and get yourself ready to stand outside and wait for that school bus to come pick you up. No use sitting around here pouting."

"Daddy!" Learline squealed, "you really mean that? I'm going to school today?"

"Book-?"

Learline's daddy held up his hand. "It's alright Bessie; I'm not going to teach my child to run away from life, no matter who's right or who's wrong. Learline's going to have to learn how to fight for herself.

Go on baby, drink your glass of milk and go on and get

yourself ready for school."

It seemed that before her daddy had gotten the words out of his mouth, Learline had finished washing up and putting on her clothes for school.

"Booker," her mother asked, "are you sure you really want us to go through all of this, this morning?"

"Y'all come on," her daddy said, "who knows what can happen. Nothing's too hard for God. Not even a bunch of hard headed white folk. If the bus comes on schedule like it's supposed to at 7:00 o'clock, it will be here in ten minutes. Y'all come on now."

Learline's daddy, her mother and her Aunt Rose all walked to the end of the street. There they stood on the corner, waiting for the school bus to come.

"Y'all think it's going to come this morning?" Mrs. Dennis, their neighbor, called out from her front porch.

"Don't know. Just going to wait and see Ada," Learline's daddy smiled.

"Mind if I wait with y'all?"

"Come on," Aunt Rose smiled, "the more, the merrier."

"What time is it now daddy?" Learline asked.

"It's 7 o'clock on the dot, sugar."

Mr. White came walking down the street with his son, Henry. Today was going to be Henry's first day in fifth grade.

"Good morning everybody," Mr. White greeted.

"Morning."

"Think they changed their minds about the schools?" he asked.

"Don't know," Learline's daddy responded, "won't hurt to stand here and wait awhile, though."

Learline looked up and down the street, searching for the big yellow school bus.

"What time is it now daddy?" she asked.

"It's thirteen minutes after seven," her daddy

responded.

A few minutes later, Jefferson, who would be starting his senior year in high school came walking toward the corner with the others.

"Morning y'all, somebody just called my grandma. They said they thought they heard the school bus riding through town. Should be on the way soon."

"Yipee," Learline cheered. "I think I hear it coming now."

Everyone got quiet and listened as the rumbling of a large automobile drove closer and closer.

"I hear it," Henry smiled.

"Me too" Learline's mother smiled and waved her hand toward the sky. "Thank you sweet Jesus."

Just then, Betty, Sally and Alberta came running through their front door into the crowd at the corner of the street.

"Wait for us they shouted."

"Wait."

"Tell him not to leave without us."

But they all looked as the white dairy truck -which wasn't a big yellow school bus -drove pass them, down the street and around the corner.

"What time is it now daddy?" Learline whined.

"Right now," her daddy looked down at his watch and then over at her mother, "it's seven forty-five."

Learline grabbed her daddy's hand. "Is the bus driver coming to pick us up for school in a few more minutes?" she asked, looking up at him.

"No," her mother answered, staring back at her father as she wiped the rolling tear from her cheek, "the bus driver is not coming by to pick y'all up for school this morning."

Learline blinked. "But why not?"

Her daddy shook his head, closed his mouth, then opened it.

"I don't have all of the answers right now for you Learline, but the one thing I can tell you is that I will not be moved. Not today. Not tomorrow. Not any day. I will not be moved."

Learline looked up at her mom and listened closely as she sang softly,

"We shall not, we shall not be moved

We shall not, we shall not be moved

Just like a tree that's standing by the water

We shall not be moved."

The others joined, singing along.

EPILOGUE

It was a crisp Monday morning on April 23, 1951, when nearly two hundred students at the Robert Russa Moton High School in Farmville (Prince Edward County), Virginia burst through its doors. Disgusted and frustrated the teenagers made the decision to strike and not return to school until the Prince Edward County School Board developed a new building for them which was equal to the all white neighboring, Farmville High School. The Moton High School strike was led by sixteen year old, Barbara Rose Johns, niece of civil rights activist Vernon Johns, the fiery preacher who preceded Rev. Dr. Martin Luther King Jr. as the pastor of Dexter Avenue Baptist Church in Montgomery, Alabama. Ms. Johns along with my father, Rev. J. Samuel Williams, Jr., John Stokes and several other students were instrumental in changing the face of American desegregation.

Historical researchers have considered this act of protest the very beginning of the integration movement in America. The student led strike, as well as four other misfortunes in the American educational system ultimately resulted in the Supreme Court Case of **Brown vs. The Board of Education**.

The U.S. Supreme Court eventually voted for Brown in 1954. The state of Virginia however responded to the mandate with an official policy of Massive Resistance. On May 1, 1959 the Prince Edward County Board of Supervisors made the harsh decision to close its schools to all students. The schools remained closed between 1959 through 1964. Prince Edward County was the only school district in the United States of America to chain its school doors for five consecutive years.

"We'd rather not have our children educated at all if they have to sit side by side with those Colored children," many said.

As a result of Massive Resistance, more than 2,000 children's lives were affected. Just as Learline's heart was broken by the news of not being able to attend school on the first day, so

were the hearts of many others; both black and white. Not only were children's lives altered, their entire families were uprooted. Some children were sent to live with distant relatives, others were taken in by strangers, yet, the majority of students were unable to relocate to other cities and states. They were needed at home to help their parents with household chores, the rearing of siblings and working local jobs. As a result of the Prince Edward County School closings many families were divided and have remained that way even until today.

Although the story, "Locked Out" is fictionalized, many children who were anticipating attending school on the first day of school in 1959 are now adults with children, grandchildren and great – grandchildren of their own.

On June 15, 2003, forty years after the official closing of the schools, four hundred adults –who were considered to be "The Lost Children" of Prince Edward County-, received honorary diplomas in the Prince Edward County High School Auditorium. Several of the 2,000 "Lost Children" had made the decision not to attend the ceremony. Others had simply refused to discuss the situation. Still many felt that the presentation of honorary awards was merely to appease them by "sweeping the school closings under the rug." Unfortunately many of the 2,000 students had already passed away.

Although my father and his classmates graduated from Robert Russa Moton High School and never entered the new high school they struck for in 1951, my sisters, cousins and several of our classmates did graduate from the new high school. Today it stands as Prince Edward County High School. As a result of the Prince Edward County School closings many misfortunes occurred. However, there were several success stories. My aunt, several other relatives and friends who were locked out of school for five years, went on to earn degrees in higher education. The so called "Lost Children" of Prince Edward County have since inspired their descendants to pursue and value the quality of a good education. Therefore, this story is a dedication to all of the "Lost Children" of Prince Edward County.

Through their courageous acts of patience, determination and perseverance, we have come to realize that if we firmly stand like trees in the troubled waters of society, "We Shall Not Be Moved."